High five from Jesus!

Hang loose from Jesus!

Thumbs up from Jesus!

I love you from Jesus!

Fist bump from Jesus!

Prayers from Jesus!

Peace from Jesus!

Heart from Jesus!

Open arms from Jesus!

Read Our Other Books

CPSIA information can be obtained
at www.ICGtesting.com
Printed in the USA
BVHW061025211020
591502BV00019B/2095